THE GERMANS IN AMERICA

THE **GERMANS** IN AMERICA

VIRGINIA BRAINARD KUNZ

Executive Secretary
Ramsey County Historical Society

Published by
Lerner Publications Company
Minneapolis, Minnesota

Fourth Printing 1969

Copyright © 1966 by Lerner Publications Company

International Copyright Secured. Printed in U.S.A.
Standard Book Number: 8225-0208-9
Library of Congress Catalog Card Number: AC 66-10147

...CONTENTS...

The Vikings discovered America 1,000 years before Columbus. They are supposed to have landed in the area now called Newfoundland. Legends tell that a German accompanied Leif Ericson on this voyage. Although the Germans did not make voyages of discovery by themselves, they did accompany the other early sea explorers.

PART I.

The Germans
in Colonial America

1. *The Background of German Settlement*

The Germans seem to have played no part in the discovery of America. The great voyages of exploration were conducted by the English, Spanish, Italians, French, and Portuguese. Yet, there is one fascinating report about what was probably the earliest voyage to America, and this story involves a man from the area of Europe now called Germany. Historians believe that Leif Ericson, a Norseman, landed in the area of Newfoundland about 1,000 years ago.

Legends of this voyage mention a German, or Teuton, named Tyrker who was one of the crew. One day Tyrker was missing. Ericson finally found him admiring the vines of wild grapes he had come upon. These vines inspired them to give the new land the name "Vinland."

Whatever the truth of the legends, five to six hundred years later, there were men and women from the Germanic states with some of the earliest expeditions which set out to establish colonies in America. Germans accompanied the French Huguenots to Florida, Captain John Smith to Jamestown, Virginia, and the Dutch to New Amsterdam.

The German people, however, were not explorers and seafarers. Germany was a loosely knit country of small states, many of them landlocked. Although the Germans stayed home during those early years of discovery, some played an important role. Among them were excellent cartographers, or mapmakers. A German mapmaker, Martin Waldseemueller, is thought to have invented the name, "America," after examining accounts of the voyages of the Italian explorer, Amerigo Vespucci.

In the early 1600's, there occurred one of those turning points in history which resulted in the emigration of the first German colonists to America. The terrible Thirty Years' War broke out in 1618. It was the result of religious conflicts which had begun 100 years earlier when Martin Luther left the Roman Catholic Church.

Germany became the battlefield for the armies of most of the European nations. They struggled back and forth across German land. When the war ended with the Treaty of Westphalia in 1648, more than half the people of Germany had died. They had been killed or had starved to death. In their misery, some of the survivors sought hope and relief in new religious sects. Many of these groups had mystical beliefs, and they were met with great disapproval by the established religions of Germany — Lutheranism, Calvinism, and Roman Catholicism. The followers of these cults were often persecuted, and they sought a place where they might be free to worship as they wanted.

These experiences of war, famine, hardship, poverty, and religious persecution drove the first German colonists to seek refuge in the New World. They came almost empty-handed, for they were poor. But they brought with them a language, customs, skills, arts, and religious and political ideas that have influenced American life from that day to this.

2. *The Beginning of German Immigration*

The first German immigrants to come to America were 13 families from Crefeld, near Holland, who sailed for the New World in 1683 on the *Concord,* called "the Mayflower of the German immigration." Under the leadership of Francis Daniel Pastorius, they founded Germantown in Pennsylvania, the first permanent German settlement in the American colonies. Pastorius had learned of America and its opportunities from William Penn, the gentle, humanitarian English Quaker who wanted to make the colony of Pennsylvania a haven for poor and oppressed people. He had traveled through the Rhineland of Germany where Crefeld is located — a once rich region plagued by depression, crop failure, famine, and high taxes — and spoke about the wonderful opportunities overseas.

Penn's report about America impressed people wherever he went. After the founding of Germantown, thousands of other Germans poured into Pennsylvania. There were an estimated 45,000 in the colony by 1745, and in 1766 Benjamin Franklin reported that the Germans made up about one-third of the entire population of Pennsylvania. While many of the German immigrants stayed in Pennsylvania during the years before the American Revolution, more passed through the colony. They followed the mountain valleys that led them southward into the back country of Maryland, Virginia, and the Carolinas.

Most of the Germans who settled in colonial America were farmers. Since they were poor, they were attracted to the frontier, or the western edge of settlement, where land was undeveloped and cheap. By the middle 1700's, Germans had settled all along the frontier, from Georgia north to the Mohawk Valley in New York, and east to the New England colonies.

3. *The Pennsylvania Dutch*

Nowhere can the contributions of German settlers to the life of colonial America be seen better than in the story of the Pennsylvania Dutch. They were not Dutch at all, of course, but Germans, and they acquired their new name in America. When English-speaking officials asked German immigrants to identify their language they answered "Deutsch," meaning German. The word was difficult for the officials to understand and soon became confused

"As the Earth Sings—Pennsylvania Dutch Family" by William Weldon Swallow (1912-1965). This pottery art work is now in the Metropolitan Museum of Art, New York.

with "Dutch." This misunderstanding was so widespread that the Pennsylvania Germans soon began to use the name "Dutch" in referring to themselves.

The Pennsylvania Dutch first settled around Philadelphia and Germantown. Later, they spread out into the eastern and southern sections of Pennsylvania, and eventually moved into Maryland, Virginia, and the South. Like all other pioneers, they had to work very hard to survive. They began life in America in sod shanties but they moved rapidly to log cabins and, eventually, to stone farmhouses. These can still be seen and are typically Pennsylvania Dutch.

The Pennsylvania Dutch were excellent farmers and soon became noted for their ambition and accomplishment. They selected wooded areas for their homesteads, knowing that these would be the best farming land. Lancaster county in southeastern Pennsylvania became known as "the farmer's paradise," and even today this area is considered the heartland of the Pennsylvania Dutch.

The most impressive building on a typical Pennsylvania Dutch farm was usually the barn. The farmers took great pride in their livestock. Their cattle were well-fed and sleek and they housed them well, rather than letting them roam the countryside. They built large, two-story barns, sometimes more than 100 feet long. These were patterned after the barns of the Black Forest region of Bavaria in southern Germany.

Most frontiersmen cleared the forests by girdling trees, counting on them to die eventually and topple over. Others cut down the trees but left the stumps in the ground until they rotted. The German farmer cleared his land completely, patiently digging out each stump. He cultivated the land thoroughly, and had a large family because children were needed to help work the land. As soon as the children were old enough, they were kept busy in the fields with hoes, mattocks, and scythes.

The German farmer made his farm as self-sufficient as possible. He grew corn, oats, rye, barley, flax, and tobacco. In addition, he usually had a garden, an orchard, and beehives. He raised nearly every type of meat animal — pigs, cows, dairy cattle, and every barnyard was alive with ducks, geese, guinea hens, and chickens. Vegetables such as cabbage and turnips which could be preserved easily, were kept through the winters in "root cellars." The Pennsylvania Germans were probably the first Americans to raise asparagus and cauliflower.

An Englishman wrote of them during the years after the American Revolutionary War:

> They are a persevering, industrious people, they cultivate the earth with care, their fields have an air of neatness about them rarely to be discovered in America. The most respectable of

them go on, adding dollar to dollar, and pack them up securely in an Iron chest. Tho' used to the habit of hiding their hard earnings they know not what to do with their money after they got it. The utmost indeavors are used to get the money, and then to keep it secret that they have got it. The men, in their leisure hours smoke, drink whiskey and water, and ride on fat horses. The women raw boned, brown skinned and barelegged, have neither grace nor beauty. They share with their husbands the labours of the field and tend about their house as menial servants.

These comments touch upon another aspect of the life of the German settlers. They were not liked and not accepted at first. Their habits, which should have been virtues, turned out to be faults. They were thrifty, to the point of being grasping and miserly. They were intensely concerned about their property, although this interest in the material things of life had more to do with good barns and fine livestock than luxuries.

Benjamin Franklin, who later came to admire them, once called them the "boors of the Palatinate" and criticized them for their lack of interest in education for their children. It must be remembered, however, that these men and women had lost almost all they had before coming to America. To make the long, dangerous journey in filthy, crowded immigrant ships, many had signed on as redemptioners. This meant that they agreed to work for a certain number of years as indentured servants to pay for their passage. They were proud of having become successful farmers in the New World. They longed for financial security, and they were very anxious to scrape together some property that could be passed on to their children, making life easier for them.

4. *The Religious Beliefs of the German Settlers*

Any account of the Germans in America must touch upon their religion. They were Protestants, and divided into many groups. It was through their faith that the heritage of these Pennsylvania Germans has been preserved and handed down through two centuries.

An Amish camp meeting. The Amish are German "sectarians." The men wear black clothing and grow beards. The women wear white caps and long gowns. They sit separately from the men.

Unlike Massachusetts or Virginia where official state churches were the rule, Pennsylvania had great freedom of religion. This attracted people of many religious beliefs, for they wanted to settle in a tolerant colony.

The Pennsylvania Dutch were divided into two major groups. One was the "church people." These belonged chiefly to the two large, established churches—the Lutheran and the Calvinist. The other Germans were called "sectarians" because they belonged to little groups, or sects, which emphasized doctrines quite different from those of the Lutherans and Calvinists. The one thing the various sectarians had in common was their emphasis on Pietism, or the religion of the heart. The central idea in Pietism is that each person can communicate directly with God, without the help of priests or churches.

Beyond this point, however, the sects did not agree. They commonly differed over ceremonials, such as baptism, and over interpretation of the Bible. The Mennonites and the Amish were the largest of the sects. Altogether, there were more than two dozen different sects, including groups named Dunkards, River Brethren, Quietists, the Mountain Men, the New Born, the Inspired, and the Society of the Woman in the Wilderness.

Through almost all of these groups ran a broad strain of mysticism. They desired to withdraw from the world, to work their land, raise their crops and children, and be left alone. Many were pacifists and conscientious objectors. They not only refused to take part in military affairs, but also rejected participation in the politics and government of their colony.

Throughout Pennsylvania the presence of a wide variety of religious faiths made it impossible for any one of them to dominate the life of the colony. Because of this, Pennsylvania offered one of the earliest examples of the division of church and state in America. This principle of tolerance, encouraged in great part by these early German settlers, has become one of the key pillars of American democracy.

Despite the numerous sectarian groups, however, the two major religious faiths of the German settlers were Lutheranism and Calvinism. These churches represented the so-called "church people," who were more worldly and less mystic. One historian has said that the most significant fact about the Pennsylvania Dutch was the fact that they were, basically, German Lutherans.

The great leader of the German Lutherans was Heinrich Melchior Muhlenberg, a towering figure in colonial America and the founder of a remarkable family which contributed greatly to the shaping of the American nation. Muhlenberg was born in Hanover, Germany, in 1711 and was educated at Gottingen and Halle. In 1742 he founded a Lutheran church in Philadelphia and by 1748 he had embarked upon his chief work, the effort to unite all the German Lutheran churches scattered over the Pennsylvania Dutch countryside into a Lutheran synod, or council. He wanted to put an end to the vagabond preachers who roamed about, visiting the small, country churches, and he wanted to be sure the churches kept the practices of their Lutheran brothers in Germany.

The leader of the German Reformed Church was the Reverend Michael Schlatter. When Schlatter first came to America in 1746, there were about 46 German Reformed congregations in all the colonies. Like Muhlenberg, he fought the "sectarians" as people who had deserted the established faith. Besides strengthening the churches and pulling them together into some sort of an overall organization, both he and Muhlenberg set up systems of parochial schools. These schools were closely associated with the churches and did much to preserve German culture and separateness in the strange, new world.

5. *Social Life and Superstitions*

The German settlers were clannish. They found it difficult to give up their native language in favor of English. Besides being divided along religious lines, the Pennsylvania Dutch were often separated into two other groups as well: the "Plain Dutch" and the "Fancy Dutch." The "Fancy Dutch" were more worldly and did not have religious scruples against material comforts. In spite of the grim struggle to exist on the frontier, these people had moments of gaiety and relaxation. They loved music and made use of it in most of their churches. Singing and instrumental music was an important part of their services.

The "Plain Dutch," who were a very small minority, clung to the traditional, conservative way of life. They can still be seen today, especially in Lancaster and Lebanon counties in Pennsylvania. It is not uncommon there to see a family of the "Plain Dutch" coming down a paved road in a black horse-drawn buggy. The women and girls wear ankle-length dresses and prayer bonnets while the men have beards and dress in wide-cut coats and trousers and flat black hats. Some of these groups even think of buttons as being ornaments and, therefore, frivolous, and so use only hooks and eyes on their clothing. As a result, they are often called "hook-and-eye Dutch." The "Plain Dutch" shun modern conveniences

Amish buggies. Neither the dress of the occupants nor the types of buggies have varied for over 100 years.

such as running water, telephones, radios, and television. If they do purchase a car, it is almost always black. They have firm ideas about education. The Amish and Mennonites, to this day, try to keep their children out of the public schools and to educate them in their own one-room schools taught by their own people.

The Germans who emigrated to the American colonies brought with them a mass of folktales and superstitions. The Pennsylvania Dutch, in particular, were famous for their superstitious nature. Many believed in witch doctors and in the use of hex signs to ward off evil spirits. These hex signs can still be seen on their houses and barns and are one of the fascinating reminders of life during the early days of the American colonies.

The Pennsylvania Dutch also believed it was bad luck to walk under a ladder and that Friday the 13th was an unlucky day. They had a good luck bird, the goldfinch, which commonly fed on thistles. In the Pennsylvania Dutch dialect, the bird was called the "Distlefink." They also believed that if one rubbed a wart with an onion, and then placed the onion under a rainspout to rot, the wart would fall off. They believed that planting should be done according to the phases of the moon, and that root vegetables such as carrots and beets should be planted between the full and the new moon.

These superstitions concerning planting led the Pennsylvania Dutch, and many other pioneers who admired their success at farming, to have great faith in farmers' almanacs which tried to forecast the weather. As a result, almanacs were among the most common forms of publications in colonial Pennsylvania. The most famous, *Poor Richard's Almanac*, was started by Benjamin Franklin in 1732. He published it for the next 25 years. Even today many almanacs are published in the Pennsylvania Dutch country.

6. *The Conestoga Wagon and "Kentucky Rifle"*

One of the most important and long-lasting contributions of the Pennsylvania Dutch to the settlement of America was the Conestoga wagon. Farmers in Germany had used small wooden carts for hauling their produce to market. But in America, where farms were bigger, farther apart, and more productive, a larger cart was needed. So the Germans developed a freight wagon called the Conestoga, after a nearby creek which had earlier been named for the Conestoga Indians.

These wagons were large and heavy. Their running gear was made from hardwoods, such as hickory, and the wagon box was usually 16 feet long, four feet wide, and four feet deep. The bottom of the box was not level, but was made to sag toward the center to keep the cargo from shifting from one side to the other.

The wagon was covered with white homespun material or canvas supported by high, arching hoops. This cover projected well over the ends of the wagon and could be drawn tight to protect the cargo from the weather. In Lancaster, where most of the wagons were made, it took four men about two months to complete a single wagon. The finished product was about 26 feet long, counting the tongue. It stood 11 feet high, weighed about 3,000 pounds and could carry from two to three tons of produce. Six big horses were needed to pull each wagon.

The Conestogas blazed with color. The canvas cover was white, the wagon box bright blue, and the wheels gleaming red. While this was certainly a patriotic color scheme, the Germans, being a practical people, actually chose it because the blue and red did not show soil.

Conestoga wagons came to have uses far beyond what their makers originally had intended. Others were quick to see their value and, in one form or another, these wagons were used throughout the United States until the end of the era of the horse-drawn vehicle. In 1755, the wagons were used for the first time outside of the Lancaster area when they carried supplies for General Braddock's campaign against the French during the French and Indian War. The American armies later used them widely during the Revolutionary War.

A covered wagon train on its way West. These modified Conestoga wagons carried the settlers who crossed the Great Plains to open up California and Oregon.

During the years of expansion and settlement after the war, the Conestoga became the most popular wagon on the frontier east of the Mississippi. Later, as the famed "covered wagons," the Conestogas helped open up the West. These were lighter than the original heavy freight wagon, and they played a vital role in the settlement of America west of the Mississippi. Conestogas carried the pioneers from the Great Plains to the Pacific Ocean.

Another major contribution of the Pennsylvania Dutch, and as vital to the history of American firearms as the Conestoga wagon was to the story of transportation, was the "Kentucky rifle." The weapon was so named because it was popularized by Kentucky's Daniel Boone and other famous frontiersmen. These men held them in high regard and gave each rifle an affectionate name, such as "Old Betsy," "Bear Killer," or "Indian Lament."

Actually, however, the rifles were developed by the Germans working away on their peaceful farms in Pennsylvania. The ordinary European musket was heavy and had a short barrel and a smooth bore, or interior. Some of these German immigrants, however, brought rifled muskets into Pennsylvania. These guns had spiral grooves on the surface of the bore. German gunsmiths correctly believed that lead balls fired from a gun would travel faster and more accurately if they were given a twist as they left the barrel.

In Pennsylvania, this German weapon was remade to suit the special needs of the hunters and trappers who carried them into the vast forests of the American continent. The first American innovation was to lengthen the barrel. This allowed the gun to deliver a more accurate and speedier bullet. The bore was then reduced in size to one-third of an inch in order to save lead, which was always in short supply on the frontier. The trigger guards on the European guns were both heavy and fancy but in the American rifles, the guards were made lighter and simpler in design. A simple type of trigger guard would not be so apt to catch on clothing or forest underbrush. The gunsights were enlarged to provide for better aim in the deep forest shade. Then the Lancaster gunsmiths added the grease patch, a piece of cloth soaked in tallow, that was wrapped around the musket ball to make it possible to load the gun more quickly and easily. All of the guns of these early years were loaded by using a ramrod to push the musket ball down the muzzle of the gun.

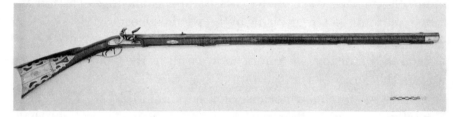

The Kentucky rifle was made in Pennsylvania, but earned its name and fame from use by frontiersmen like Kentucky's Daniel Boone.

The completed rifle weighed from seven to nine pounds and was nearly five feet long. In the hands of a sharpshooter, the gun was accurate up to 300 yards. The metal parts were handmade. Both the metal and the wood stock were usually adorned with intricate hand-carvings. Stocks sometimes were decorated with brass and silver inlays, so that the finished product was artistic as well as useful.

These Pennsylvania-made rifles were used during the American Revolutionary War and were in great demand on the frontier. Pioneering settlers not only hunted their own game but often had to protect their homes from Indian attack. Most of Major General Andrew Jackson's Tennessee and Kentucky militiamen used Kentucky rifles at the Battle of New Orleans during the War of 1812. This rifle later became the model for many other famous guns of the West.

7. *The Valley of the Mohawk*

The Pennsylvania Dutch were not the only Germans who came to America before the Revolutionary War. There was at least one other large and important group of German immigrants in that period and for their story we move into what is now New York State.

About 10 miles north of the site of present-day Albany, the capital of New York, the Mohawk River flows into the Hudson River. More than 200 years ago, German immigrants settled in this area, which was then the headquarters of the famed Six Nations, a confederation of Iroquois Indian tribes.

The settlers had come to the New York colony in the early 1700's. They formed the largest single immigrant group in America during the years before the Revolutionary War. Their European home had been the Palatinate, a section of southwestern Germany along the Rhine River, and they were encouraged to emigrate by the British government. During the reign of Queen Anne, the English began to actively promote the settlement of New York by the Germans as part of a plan to produce supplies for the British Navy.

The British paid the transportation and settlement expenses of these German immigrants but they went as redemptioners. They were like indentured servants, pledged to produce for the British Navy until all the money spent on them had been paid off. So many were attracted by this offer that the British soon tried to shut off the flow.

The first group came down the Rhine in 1708 under the leadership of Joshua Kocherthal. Their immediate destination was Holland, where they waited for transportation, first to England and then to the colonies. By the next year, 4,000 immigrants from the Palatinate were arriving in Holland each month. Their journey took four to six weeks. Many had no money or food and survived only with the help of people along the way.

In 1709, Joshua Kocherthal's group of refugees had founded Neuberg, now Newburgh, on the Hudson River north of New York City. By 1711, the British government had spent more than 100,000 pounds to establish seven villages of German settlers on the land grant of Robert Livingston. In the next years, the German immigrants began to move north. By 1713, some 50 families were living in the Schoharie River Valley south of present-day Schenectady and others had moved into the lovely Mohawk River Valley. For many years, this entire region was known as the "German flats" and noted as excellent farming country, in spite of Indian raids. The Germans prospered in New York as they did in Pennsylvania. By 1750, they had built about 500 houses, mostly of stone, on a 12-mile strip along the Mohawk.

8. *Prominent Germans of Colonial America*

Numbered among the Germans of colonial America were some remarkable men. One outstanding German immigrant of this early period was John Peter Zenger, who became famous as the man who fought for the principle of freedom of the press. Zenger was born in Germany in 1697 and came to America when he was 13 years old. His parents died during the voyage and Zenger was apprenticed even before setting foot in the New World. Through his apprenticeship he learned the printing business, and in 1726 he set up a printing shop of his own.

Zenger's career in journalism began when the governor of New York, William Cosby, removed Chief Justice Lewis Morris from office. This act was resented by many of New York's citizens. Morris and some of his supporters established a newspaper, the *New York Weekly Journal,* with Zenger as editor. The newspaper soon began printing articles which were highly critical of the governor. Although Zenger's powerful friends probably wrote the critical articles, Zenger, as publisher of the paper, was legally responsible.

In 1734, Zenger was arrested and held in jail for 10 months awaiting trial on charges of criminal libel. This is the crime of printing something with the intent to injure or defame another person. Zenger was defended by a renowned lawyer of the time, Andrew Hamilton of Philadelphia. Hamilton argued that the newspaper criticism of Cosby was not unlawful because the statements were true. Zenger was acquitted and he will always be remembered for

The first page of the first issue of *The New York Weekly Journal,* edited by John Peter Zenger. Notice the date: Monday, November 5, 1733. This newspaper helped establish one of our most cherished principles, freedom of the press.

this famous case which contributed so much to the principles of freedom of expression in America.

Among other prominent German immigrants was Christian Priber, an idealist with a vision. He had been born in Saxony, lived in England, and came to South Carolina in the 1730's. He was a learned man who wanted to establish a perfect state, a republic called "Paradise."

Priber crossed the Smoky Mountains and traveled 500 miles into what then was wild Indian country. His ideas were so convincing to the Indian chiefs he met and the few white men living there that he actually came very close to organizing a movement. The French and the British on the frontier decided he was dangerous and imprisoned him for the rest of his long life in a British fort on St. Simon Island off the coast of Georgia. Apparently Priber never lost his belief that America had the makings of a Utopia. He eventually came to be admired and his ideas respected by his captors.

There are many "firsts" among the Germans who came to America during the earliest years. In 1690, William Rittinghausen set up America's first paper mill at Germantown. Caspar Wistar was the founder of the glassmaking industry in America. In 1739, he built a plant in Salem, New Jersey, which he operated until 1781. Wistar is recognized today as one of the great names of early American glass.

The second great name among American glassmakers also belongs to a German immigrant, Henry William Stiegel. He was born near Cologne, Germany, in 1729. Stiegel laid out the town of Manheim in Pennsylvania and between 1764 and 1773 made some of the most beautiful glass seen in America. He used rare colors and raised decorations. But the Revolutionary War cost him his business and he died in poverty.

Another famous German was Christopher Saur of Germantown who, in 1743, published a German-language Bible, the first Bible to be printed in the American colonies. He also was the publisher of the first religious magazine in America. In 1771, his son founded the first foundry for making type in North America.

PART II.

The American Revolution

1. *Patriots, Tories, and Conscientious Objectors*

The days of British rule over her American colonies were drawing to an end. Talk of political and economic freedom from Great Britain was rising all along the Atlantic seaboard. Britain's desire to govern and tax her colonies as she saw fit and the colonies' wish to govern themselves were ideas which were bound to clash. And clash they did. The fuse was lit with the Boston Massacre and the explosion came with the fighting at Lexington and Concord in Massachusetts. The 300,000 Germans, who now made up about 10 percent of the entire colonial population, were to play an important part in the American Revolution.

The struggle for independence, which divided the colonists into patriots and loyalists, or Tories, sharply split the German immigrants. The "sectarians," those who belonged to the many small religious sects which lay outside the established churches of the Germans, were strong pacifists and refused to do military service. Most colonies, however, regarded them as conscientious objectors and allowed them to either send someone to fight in their place or to pay special taxes.

Many of these Germans who refused to take up arms served in their own way. Some took care of soldiers in their homes or furnished supplies to General George Washington's army. Throughout the terrible winter at Valley Forge, it was men such as these German farmers of Pennsylvania who kept the army from starving by getting supplies to the tired soldiers. Others set up hospitals and served in them. The Moravians from Bethlehem, Pennsylvania, tended the men at Valley Forge. They were members of the Moravian Church, a Protestant sect which had sent missionaries from Germany to the American colonies in 1741. After the Battle of Brandywine, a group of German pacifists set up and staffed a hospital in a nearby schoolhouse.

Although in some areas the Germans' refusal to enter military service was respected by their patriotic neighbors, it was not so in all places. Some Germans were shunned and even banished. This was, for the most part, because they refused to take an oath of allegiance to the Revolutionary government. Some German settlers lost everything. Christopher Saur was an example. He was a pacifist who continued to express his views against the war in his newspaper. His sons became Tories. His family remained loyal to the British cause and moved to Nova Scotia. In 1778, the colonial government took over all their property. They had, by this time, become a wealthy family, and one of the oldest German families in America. They were among a number of German immigrants who paid dearly for their devotion to England.

The German church people, those who belonged to the German Lutheran or German Reformed churches, did not share the sectarians' objections to military service. From these church people, almost all of them loyal to the Revolutionary government, came some of the great heroes of the war.

The great majority of the Mohawk Valley Germans were intensely patriotic. Much of this feeling came from their resentment against the way they had been treated by the settlers who were of English ancestry. Many of the English seemed to regard Germans as outlandish and peculiar. In the Mohawk Valley, in particular, the Germans had been under the rule of wealthy English landowners, such as Sir William Johnson. These Mohawk Germans were for anyone who was against the British. In 1774, a year before the Revolutionary War began, the Germans of the Mohawk Valley issued their own "declaration of independence." In it they said they would die rather than live under tyranny and oppression.

2. *The German Role in the Revolutionary War*

After the Battle of Lexington in April 1775, the opening battle of the war, a volunteer company known as the German Fusileers was formed in Charleston, South Carolina. Two months later, after the Battle of Bunker Hill, four companies of infantry were formed from among the Germans living around Reading, Pennsylvania. The cavalry troops commanded by Count Casimir Pulaski were made up almost entirely of Germans from the area around Bethlehem, Pennsylvania. The Count, however, was Polish.

An entire German regiment was raised in Pennsylvania and Maryland and the men fought under the command of Nikolas Haussegger and Ludwig Weltner. They took part in the campaigns in New Jersey.

In the spring of 1775, about the time of the first fighting at Lexington and Concord, the Mohawk Germans set up a Committee of Safety in Tyron County. Under this committee, four battalions were recruited and three years later they played an important role in the war in the Battle of Oriskany.

In 1777, a British force under General Barry Saint Leger tried to link up with another British army coming from Canada and led by British Major General John Burgoyne. The meeting place was to be Albany, New York. Saint Leger got as far as Fort Stanwix, a dilapidated fort on the Mohawk River which was held by the colonial army. Saint Leger laid siege to the fort, which was defended stubbornly by the 750 men inside.

The four battalions of Tyron County under the command of Brigadier General Nicholas Herkimer, a veteran of the French and

Indian War, marched up the Mohawk Valley to assist Fort Stanwix. Near Oriskany, Herkimer's force was ambushed in a ravine. The battle raged all day long, and at twilight Herkimer ordered his men to retreat. He had been wounded and died 11 days later.

Despite the retreat, the Battle of Oriskany on August 6, 1777, proved to be one of the decisive actions of the war. The British and their Indian allies had been so badly mauled that they retreated from Fort Stanwix to their base farther west at Oswego. Thus, they were unable to reach General Burgoyne. Three months later, Burgoyne, trapped near Saratoga, surrendered his army of more than 5,000 men to the American commander, General Horatio Gates. News of Burgoyne's surrender, made possible in part by those German battalions which stopped Saint Leger, crossed the

John Peter Gabriel Muhlenberg (1746-1807). The son of a German immigrant, he was born at Trappe, Pennsylvania, and became a Lutheran minister. One dramatic Sunday morning in 1776 while preaching at Woodstock, Virginia, he removed his minister's robes to show his colonel's uniform underneath. He raised a German regiment to fight for the American Revolution. After the war, he was a representative in Congress for three terms.

Baron de Kalb, who was born in Bavaria, died at the battle of Camden while fighting on the side of the Americans in the Revolutionary War.

wide Atlantic to France and helped the French government make up its mind to enter the war on the side of the Americans.

Other distinguished Germans served the patriot cause in many ways during the Revolutionary War. Washington trusted the German colonists and selected a number of them for his bodyguard, a group commanded by Major Barth von Heer. Heinrich Emmanuel Lutterloh was quartermaster general of the American Army and Christopher Ludwig had charge of the bakeries which supplied the army. He was paid $75 a month.

Peter Muhlenberg, son of the famous founder of the German-Lutheran Church in America, was also a German-Lutheran pastor. On a Sunday morning in 1776, he ended his sermon by saying: "There is a time for preaching and praying, but also a time for battle, and such a time has now arrived." Standing there in the pulpit before his congregation, he removed his pastor's robes. Underneath them he was wearing the uniform of a colonel in the Continental Army. He later became a general and fought in the battles of Brandywine, Germantown, and Yorktown.

Baron de Kalb, a soldier of fortune who was born in Bavaria, Germany, came to America with the Marquis de Lafayette. He became a sincere patriot and died bravely at the Battle of Camden

The Von Steuben commemerative, issued to honor the 200th anniversary of the birth of this German-born general who became one of George Washington's principal aides.

in South Carolina. He had been born a commoner, rose to the rank of general in the French Army, and added the title of baron to his name upon arriving in America.

A genuine German baron made one of the greatest military contributions to the American cause. Baron Friedrich Wilhelm von Steuben was the son of a Prussian army officer and entered the Prussian officer corps when he was 17. During the Seven Years' War he was an aide to King Frederick the Great and also served on the Prussian general staff.

Von Steuben was highly regarded as a military strategist by the time he was discharged in 1763. For the next 12 years, he held court positions for various German princes. In 1776, he had financial difficulties because of the bankruptcy of his employer. After trying unsuccessfully to enter the Austrian Army, he went to Paris where he met Benjamin Franklin who felt at once that Von Steuben would be of great help to Washington. Von Steuben was actually a captain, on half-pay, and not a lieutenant general as his record stated. Franklin, however, who apparently wanted to impress the Continental Congress, seems to have promoted Von Steuben and sent him off to America. Von Steuben arrived while Washington was suffering with his troops through the winter at Valley Forge and the Prussian was ordered to join him.

Von Steuben at once began the hard, grinding task of turning the shivering, tattered, footsore men into a disciplined, well-functioning army. He toiled from dawn to dusk against great difficulties. He spoke very little English and some French, so he

Von Steuben drilling troops at Valley Forge. During the long winter at Valley Forge (1777-1778), Von Steuben converted the tattered, weary soldiers into a well-disciplined army. Because he was unable to speak English, other officers had to translate Von Steuben's orders to his men.

worked out a system whereby, through the use of other officers as interpreters, his orders were translated from German into French into English. Yet, he managed to establish a comradeship with the men whom he shaped into a true fighting force.

Von Steuben introduced a discipline that soon was copied throughout the army. In 1778 and 1779 he wrote a pamphlet on military regulations, popularly called the "blue book." It became the standard army instruction manual.

While famed as an instructor and drillmaster, Von Steuben also had a shrewd knowledge of military tactics. He was of great value at the Battle of Yorktown where the colonists attacked a fixed British position. Von Steuben was the only member of Washington's staff who was familiar with siege tactics and his advice was closely followed in the successful assault.

The USS Von Steuben, a nuclear submarine named
in honor of the Revolutionary War hero.

After the Revolutionary War, Von Steuben became an American
citizen. Four states voted him grants of land and he was given a
pension by Congress. He spent his remaining years in New York
where he was active in veterans' organizations and the German
Society of New York. He also served as a regent of the University
of New York.

One of the best known stories of the Revolutionary War con-
cerns the young woman called "Molly Pitcher," who was the heroine
of the Battle of Monmouth. "Molly" was the daughter of German
immigrants and had been born near Trenton, New Jersey. Her real
name was Maria Ludwig and she married a man named John Casper
Hays. After the war began, her husband enlisted as a gunner in the
First Pennsylvania Artillery and went into camp at Valley Forge
with the rest of Washington's troops.

Like Martha Washington and the wives of many other soldiers,
Molly Pitcher joined her husband in camp to cook, wash clothes,

Maria Ludwig, the daughter of
German immigrants, is known in
American history as "Molly Pitcher."

and help where she was needed. She was with the army when the Battle of Monmouth was fought on Sunday, June 28, 1778. The day was extremely hot and Molly carried pitchers of water to the fighting men to help ease their thirst. This, of course, is how she came to be called Molly Pitcher.

During the battle, her husband was wounded and Molly took his place, firing his cannon throughout the rest of the battle. She survived the war by more than 50 years. In 1822, the Pennsylvania state legislature awarded her an annual pension of $40.

3. *The Hessians*

One group of Germans in the Revolutionary War period fought on the British side. These were the mercenaries, or paid soldiers, called Hessians. Although brought here to fight, many remained as settlers.

When the war began, Great Britain had a small army and found it difficult to recruit soldiers for service in the colonies. Therefore, King George III and his advisors decided to hire troops. Treaties were drawn up with a number of petty German rulers who agreed to furnish so many soldiers per year at so much a head.

The German troops came from six of the German states — Brunswick, Hesse-Cassel, Hesse-Hanau, Waldeck, Anspack-Bayreuth, and Anhalt-Zerbst. Eventually, 30,000 German soldiers were sent to the colonies during the war. More than half of these came from Hesse-Cassel, so the term "Hessian" came into general use to describe a German mercenary.

Of these 30,000, an estimated 12,000 stayed behind to make their homes in the new United States. Early in the war, the Continental Congress began a campaign to lure the Hessians from the British. They were promised all the rights of American settlers, plus grants of land ranging from 50 acres for a common soldier to much larger grants for officers.

Some 5,000 Hessians deserted to the American side during the war, finding help and shelter with friendly German patriots who

General George A. Custer, the descendant of a Hessian soldier named Kuester. Custer was a distinguished Union officer during the Civil War. He is here shown in front of a Northern Pacific Railroad tent (notice the tent markings) with some scouts. His 7th Regiment was then guarding Northern Pacific construction crews in the Dakota territory. Custer and his entire command were killed shortly after by Sioux Indians at the battle of the Little Big Horn (Montana) on June 25, 1876.

recognized the ties of kinship. The German-Americans realized that the "foreigners" had very little choice when ordered to serve by the ruler of their German state. At any rate, there seems to have been little ill-will between the "native" German-Americans and the Hessians. At the end of the war two states, South Carolina and New Jersey, sent out pamphlets in German urging the Hessians to stay in America and take up land. Some of the Hessian prisoners of war in Pennsylvania and Virginia were helped by German-Americans to escape to the west. These men were among the first pioneers to cross the Allegheny Mountains.

One Hessian soldier named Kuester settled in Pennsylvania. The spelling of his name was changed over the years, but he was the first American ancestor of General George Custer who was massacred 100 years later with his men during a battle with the Sioux Indians on the Little Big Horn River in Montana.

4. *The Early Years of the Republic*

The end of the Revolutionary War came officially with the Treaty of Paris of 1783. By 1790, the Germans numbered about 360,000 in a total white population of 3,172,000. They farmed industriously. The artisans among them ran their businesses and maintained their reputations as skilled craftsmen and hard, steady, dependable workers. They were people who gave the new country a stability which was sorely needed during the first trying years. Publication of books and newspapers in the German language flourished, as did early choral societies, reflecting the German love for music. All the elements of the culture that later German immigrants would bring to the United States were beginning to be seen during the early years of the republic.

Although most Germans did not take an active role in politics, there were some exceptions. Frederick Muhlenberg, another member of that remarkable Pennsylvania Dutch family, was chosen the first speaker of the House of Representatives and was twice re-elected. He was in office when Congress adopted the first 10 amendments to the Constitution, known as the Bill of Rights, and they carry his signature.

Frederick Augustus Conrad Muhlenberg, (1750-1801), the brother of John Peter Gabriel Muhlenberg. He was a Revolutionary War patriot from a family of patriots. Like his father and brother, he was a Lutheran minister. His political service included membership in the Continental Congress and the House of Representatives.

The Bill of Rights (1789). The first ten amendments to the Constitution guarantee such fundamental American principles as freedom of speech, freedom of religion, and freedom of the press. This document is the joint resolution of Congress of September 25, 1789, proposing 12 amendments. Ten were ratified and became part of the Constitution in 1791. The resolution was signed by Frederick Augustus Muhlenberg, Speaker of the House of Representatives, and John Adams, Vice-President of the United States.

Johann Adam Treutlen was the first governor of Georgia. Heinrich Miller was Congress' first printer. His newspaper, the *Philadelphia Staatsbote*, had been first in the colonies to announce the adoption of the Declaration of Independence. Michael Hillegas, who was of German and French Huguenot ancestry, was the first treasurer of the United States.

One of American history's most famous self-made businessmen, John Jacob Astor, came to the United States in 1783 when he was 20 years of age. His father was a ne'er-do-well butcher and the son had little schooling. During his voyage to the United States, however, he chanced to meet a fur trader and by the time Astor had landed he had chosen his career.

For a time, he traded in furs and sold musical instruments. He had brought seven flutes with him to America. By 1800, Astor had

John Jacob Astor, a German immigrant who became the wealthiest man of early 19th century America. His fortune was made in fur trading and real estate.

amassed a fortune of about a quarter of a million dollars — a remarkable accomplishment for a man who had only $25 and seven flutes 17 years earlier.

At a point where many would have been content, Astor pushed on. In 1808 he organized the American Fur Company. The company boomed with the expanding fur trade after the War of 1812. In the meantime, Astor began investing in New York real estate, which proved to be highly profitable. By the late 1820's, the American Fur Company had become the leading trader in the Great Lakes and the Rocky Mountain areas.

Astor sold out in 1834 when he decided the fur trade was a dying business. At the time of his death, he was said to have been worth $20,000,000, and to be the richest man in the country. His founding of Astoria, which was originally a fur trading post on the Pacific Ocean, marked the real beginning of the settlement of what is now the State of Oregon.

The Astor Column in Astoria, Oregon. John Jacob Astor's fur trading post in Astoria marked the beginning of settlement in the Northwest. A frieze spiraling upward on the tower shows the important events in the history of the territory.

PART III.

German Settlers of the 19th Century

1. *The Flood of New Immigrants*

During the last years of the 18th century and the early years of the 19th century, immigration to the United States, including that of the Germans, fell off sharply. Earlier, the Revolutionary War, with its political and military turmoil, discouraged would-be immigrants. Then, after the American Revolution, western Europe was occupied with the French Revolution and its consequences. Because they were fighting wars with France, many German rulers would not let men leave the country. They were needed for German armies.

Since skilled German craftsmen were also needed at home, many German states issued special decrees forbidding them to leave the country. Nevertheless, they did leave. One emigrant, a glassblower from Hanover, had himself smuggled out as a corpse in a coffin. Then he traveled to Maryland where a glassmaker, whose labor agent had recruited him, needed his special talents.

Many Americans went to Germany during these years of the early 1800's to find workers for jobs in America. Some of the newly

German emigrants embarking for New York on a Hamburg steamer. During the last half of the 19th century, German immigration to the United States exceeded that of any other country. Faster, less expensive steamship travel was partly responsible for the increased immigration during these years.

created states, such as Ohio, began to follow the example of William Penn and advertise the availability of their vast, rich farmlands. German immigration then began to rise. In 1832 it passed 10,000. By 1834, the figure had jumped to 17,000, and by 1837 to 24,000.

From 1820 to 1900, about five million Germans came into the United States. In fact, during the last half of the 19th century, German immigration exceeded that of any other single country. Throughout the century German immigrants arrived in ships which landed at every major American port, including New Orleans, Louisiana. Although many immigrants remained in the eastern part of the United States, thousands upon thousands headed for the Middle West and, eventually the West and the Southwest. They traveled in long immigrant trains, and they came up the river from New Orleans to settle the Mississippi Valley.

GERMAN IMMIGRATION IN THE 19TH CENTURY

1820	968
1821-1830	6,761
1831-1840	152,454
1841-1850	434,626
1851-1860	951,667
1861-1870	787,468
1871-1880	718,182
1881-1890	1,452,970
1891-1900	505,152

The German immigrants added to the growth of what are today some of America's leading cities — cities which still have a large German population: Rochester and Buffalo, New York; Cincinnati and Cleveland, Ohio; St. Louis, Missouri, and Milwaukee, Wisconsin. Artisans and craftsmen tended to choose the life of the towns, where they could establish their businesses. They were in great demand and had no difficulty getting jobs because the Industrial Revolution was in full swing in America and industries were growing rapidly. These German craftsmen helped along this industrial expansion because they had been well-trained under the

A typical 19th century immigrant from Bavaria, then one of several small independent German states.

old guild system of apprentices. And they transplanted to America the European system of guilds, whereby men with the same skills formed their own organization. This was the beginning of the trade union movement which later resulted in the American Federation of Labor, an organization of unions based upon individual crafts.

These workingmen's unions were quite common in America's industrial centers during and after the 1830's. It was the Germans who in the 1850's helped these little groups unite into larger unions, thus strengthening their bargaining position and helping to obtain such benefits as better hours, improved working conditions, and insurance benefits.

There is no doubt that most of the Germans of the 19th century came to the United States to improve themselves economically. Of course, not all of them were craftsmen. Thousands upon thousands of them were farmers, but they, too, like most of the other German immigrants of the 19th century, were drawn by the economic opportunities America offered. Cheap, good land was the great attraction for the German farmers. Land was selling for $2 or $3 an acre in the newly opened areas and, after the passage of the Homestead Act in 1862, land was available practically free to any applicant for citizenship. Some groups of immigrants sent agents out ahead of them to select the best farming areas.

By the middle of the 19th century, German immigration to the United States was in full swing. By 1860, Germans accounted for nearly one-third of the total number of foreign-born residents in the United States. Between 1845 and 1861 alone, 1,250,000 German immigrants landed in America. Newspapers of those years were full of stories and notices concerning arrivals of these immigrants and of the long immigrant trains which rumbled across the American countryside.

In part, the flood of immigration was helped by improvements in ocean transportation. By the 1850's, steamships generally had replaced sailing vessels and the steam-driven ships reduced the ocean voyage from six weeks to two. They also made cheaper fares possible. In the United States, steamboats on the main rivers, such

A wagon train on the Oregon Trail. Many German immigrants took the long dangerous journey to Oregon. Approximately 25 percent of that state's residents are descended from German immigrants.

as the Ohio and the Mississippi, made movement easier for the immigrants. By 1860, several railroads linked the major cities of the east coast with the Mississippi River and it was along these railroad lines that the immigrant trains passed. By 1869, it had become possible to cross the entire country by rail. As a result, immigrants could move farther, faster, and cheaper than ever before.

Germans were represented in all areas of the country and took part in the major events of the 19th century in America. Some groups went to Texas when it was the Lone Star Republic, and then became American citizens after Texas was annexed to the United States in 1845. Many other Germans followed the move westward and participated in the California Gold Rush or the long trek to Oregon. There were instances of Germans moving west in groups of "colonies" and forming towns. Examples of this are found in Texas, Colorado, and Minnesota. One of these towns, New Ulm, Minnesota, became famous through a tragic event of the mid-19th century. New Ulm was established by organized German groups before the Civil War. These German settlers bore the brunt of the Sioux Uprising of 1862, one of the bloodiest Indian wars in American history.

The end of the Civil War ushered in an immense wave of immigration from Germany. The story of this phase of German immigration is not much different from the story of other immigrant groups of the period, except that more people were involved. By 1900, nearly 2,700,000 Germans who had been born in Europe were living in the United States. The Germans began to emigrate by the tens and hundreds of thousands in 1870, the year the Franco-Prussian War began. The immigrants fled to avoid war, conscription, or forced military service, and the harshness of the Prussian drive to unite the small German states into one country.

Many of them were also influenced by the careers in America of outstanding German-born Americans. During the latter part of the 19th century there were more than 700 newspapers published in America in the German language. Copies of these papers found their way to Europe where Germans could read in great detail of the activities of important German-Americans. Letters written back home by Germans settled in the United States telling of the opportunities open to foreigners also served to influence many new immigrants.

Large numbers of peasants came to the United States to farm the rich lands available to them under the Homestead Act. Somewhat later in the last years of the 1800's, the character of the German immigration changed. More craftsmen and industrial workers entered the country, rather than farmers. Even so, according to the United States census of 1900, the great majority of the farming in America was still being done by Germans. These figures show that there were 522,252 farmers who were either German-born or descended from earlier German immigrants. This is compared with 183,157 farmers of Anglo-Saxon origin and 174,694 farmers from Scandinavian countries.

2. The "Forty-Eighters"

A small but very significant and important number of Germans left Europe for political reasons. The years between 1830 and

With the development of the transcontinental railroad in 1869, immigrants could travel faster, cheaper, and safer than before. This is a scene of recently arrived immigrants in the waiting-room of the Union Pacific Railroad depot at Omaha, Nebraska.

1848 were an era of political upheaval. The many rulers of the small German states were engaged in suppressing the democratic ideas which had been released by the French Revolution. But these liberal ideals lived on among the educated. They wanted a united Germany with a republican system of government and political equality for everyone.

Revolutions aimed at achieving these goals broke out in Germany in 1830 and 1848. These revolutions were failures and their leaders, and others who felt they could not live under the tyranny of the German ruling classes, fled to America — some of the revolutionaries fleeing for their lives.

These political refugees were called the "Forty-Eighters" and among them were outstanding German-Americans. They were men of excellent training, education, and social standing. For many years to come they provided leadership in the German communities in the United States, and made important and long-lasting contributions to American life, culture, and institutions.

Although the United States was a democracy, it was still not a perfect government. There were dishonest politicians, and people who used government for selfish purposes. Some political leaders used the words of democracy only to conceal their abuse of public office for their own self-interest. The "Forty-Eighters" were idealists who found much to criticize. They attacked the rowdiness of American politics. They opposed American Puritanism and the strictness of the Sabbath, which they regarded as a limitation of personal liberty.

For some years, these German reformers were very outspoken in their criticism and sought to improve American ways. Some had plans to create a separate German state in America. Their most powerful spokesmen were often newspaper editors, frequently of German-language newspapers. There was Wilhelm Weber, editor and owner of the *St. Louis Anzeiger des Westens;* Friedrich Hassaurek, editor of the influential *Volksblatt* in Cincinnati; Oswald Ottendorfer, owner of the *New York Staats Zeitung,* and Hermann R. Rastner, editor of the *Buffalo Democrat.*

This criticism of America, sometimes stressing the bad points and overlooking the good, aroused unfriendly reaction against German immigrants among some Americans. The situation helped create a political party called the "Know-Nothings." It was more of a collection of secret societies than a political party, but it was influential in American politics during the early years of the 1850's. It opposed immigration and "foreigners" in public office. During its period of existence, various groups, among which were the Germans and the Irish, were subjected to abuse, mistreatment, and persecution.

The more radical of these reformers also caused a great deal of controversy within the German-American community. The older members had come to America many years earlier. They cared nothing for sweeping reforms or for wild schemes like a separate German state in America. A fierce war-of-words raged among the German language newspapers. The older groups tried to hold the newer immigrants in check. Some of the "Forty-Eighters" became disillusioned and returned to Germany. But most began to adjust to life in America. With the agitation in the North for the abolition of slavery, they found a cause to which they could devote their energies.

In spite of their faults, these German intellectuals who came to the United States during the years before the Civil War were one of the most valuable groups of 19th century immigrants. Like most immigrants, they at first worked at whatever jobs they could find. They farmed, dug canals, and heaved picks to build railroads. It was not unusual to hear them recite Latin and Greek as they worked. This resulted in their being named "Latin" farmers. Eventually, however, most of them found places in the professions for which they had been trained.

Among these immigrants was Gustav Korner who settled in Belleville, Illinois, which was a typical settlement of "Latin" farmers. Korner became active in the Democratic party and rose to be a judge on the Illinois Supreme Court. He joined the Republican party soon after its founding in 1854 and was later elected lieutenant governor of Illinois. In 1862, he was appointed United States minister to Spain.

Friedrich Munch, who had studied philosophy in Germany, settled down as a farmer in Missouri. Later, he moved to newspaper work and wrote philosophical essays and novels.

Carl Schurz is the "Forty-Eighter" who became one of the most famous German immigrants in American history. He had studied to be a history professor, but was forced to abandon his career because of involvement in the Revolution of 1848. He came to the United States in 1852, a young man in his mid-twenties with a temper that matched his bristling red beard.

Schurz settled on a farm near Watertown, Wisconsin. Wisconsin, Minnesota, and Missouri were three states where "Forty-Eighters" hoped to set up a "New Germany." But Schurz had little patience with the idea of a German state within a state, and felt that the future of the German immigrants was completely tied to the future of the United States and not to a separate German country. He quickly learned English and became a devoted, patriotic American. An ardent opponent of slavery, he soon was active in the new Republican party. He became a warm, personal friend of Abraham Lincoln, for whom he compaigned hard in 1860. His influence with German-speaking voters was of great help. President Lincoln appointed him United States minister to Spain in

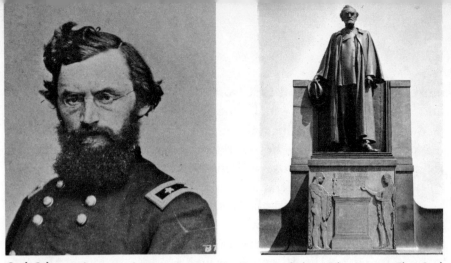

Carl Schurz, the most famous German immigrant of the 19th century. The Carl Schurz Memorial in New York City (right) has engraved on its base: "A Defender of Liberty and a Friend of Human Rights."

1861, but Schurz came home in 1862 and enlisted in the Union Army. During the Civil War, he distinguished himself in several engagements, including the Battle of Gettysburg. He had risen to the rank of major general by the end of the war.

After the war, Schurz made his home in St. Louis, Missouri, where he edited a German-language newspaper. He delivered the keynote address at the 1868 Republican convention and the next year he was chosen a United States Senator from the State of Missouri.

In 1877 he was named Secretary of the Interior by President Hayes. In this position, Schurz championed a humane policy regarding the treatment of the American Indians, introduced the merit system in the Interior Department, and advocated preservation of public lands. After 1881, his career was mainly journalistic. He was an editor of the *New York Evening Post* and *Harper's Weekly*. He also served as president of the National Civil Service Reform League.

3. *The Civil War*

One of the most interesting and inspiring aspects of American history is the role played by the Germans in the nation's wars.

48

They came to the American colonies originally to escape the sufferings of European wars. Later, large numbers came partly to escape forced service in the armies of the German states. They were primarily peaceful folk who wanted to run their farms or shops and be left alone. Yet, they turned out in great numbers to fight loyally and bravely in every war of their adopted country.

During the War Between the States, German-Americans fought in both the Union and Confederate armies. One historian estimates that 176,817 soldiers in the Union Army had been born in Germany. Other estimates are as high as 216,000. The number of Union soldiers who were American-born but of German ancestry seems to be a matter of an "educated guess," but one writer puts the number at about 300,000.

At least 500 officers of the Union Army were born in Germany. Among them were nine major generals and several brigadier generals. The most distinguished included Carl Schurz, Franz Sigel, Ludwig Blenker, Adolf V. Steinwehr, Peter J. Osterhaus, Gottfried Weitzel, August Willich, Friedrich Hecker, August B. Kautz, Gustav Struve, Alexander Schimmelpfennig, Julius Stahl, Max Weber, Hubert Dilger, and August Moor. General William Rosecrans was American-born, but of German descent.

Upon President Lincoln's first call for volunteers after the fall of Fort Sumter, an estimated 4,000 Germans in Pennsylvania and

Major General Peter J. Osterhaus (left), one of over 500 officers of the Union Army who were born in Germany. **General Franz Sigel** (right), another German-born Union general, helped save Missouri for the Union.

6,000 in New York joined up. Entire regiments were formed of German volunteers. Many could not speak English so commands were given in German. Of course, the "Forty-Eighters" with their hatred of slavery, helped lead the Germans of the North into the war. It was not entirely easy, particularly among the farmers of the Middle Western states who were not really concerned with either the abolition of slavery or the preservation of the Union. They volunteered for service very slowly, if at all. There were anti-draft riots in Wisconsin. The German "sectarians" in the North who were pacifists were excused from active military duty on the grounds of conscientious objections. Some were allowed to make a financial payment. Others worked in non-combatant jobs as teamsters or as hospital orderlies.

The devotion of the German population of Missouri helped save that state for the Union, for the governor of the state was much opposed to Lincoln and his policies. The Germans living in St. Louis and surrounding counties raised an artillery regiment, four German infantry regiments, and a home guard made up of 3,000 Germans commanded by Colonel H. Almstedt. In May of 1861, the German troops joined with a small group of army regulars to seize Confederate Camp Jackson. A 10-month campaign followed. Under the command of General Franz Sigel, many Germans distinguished themselves. The next spring, the governor and his forces were defeated and Missouri remained with the North.

The large number of foreign-born soldiers in the Union Army aroused some controversy over the use of "foreign troops." This was a carry-over of the hostility to new immigrants that had been the program of the "Know-Nothings." General Blenker's brigade, whose officers were all German and gave their commands in German, came out intact after the disastrous first Battle of Bull Run. But he was criticized for allowing the sale of beer to his troops. The Germans under Colonel August Willich fought bravely at Shiloh. The defeat of the Union forces at Chancellorsville, however, where Carl Schurz's division was beaten back, aroused a storm of debate over the worth of the German troops. This controversy continued

Union generals **Louis Blenker** (left) and **August Willich** (right) were both German-born, as were seven other Union major generals.

even though Schurz and Franz Sigel had done well at the second Battle of Bull Run.

At Gettysburg, Schurz's troops again had to retreat, although they had fought well. Each setback brought cries of "cowardice" from those who looked for scapegoats, and were ready to blame the immigrant-American when anything went wrong.

The Confederacy had its German troops too. There were six German companies in one of the Louisiana regiments and Georgia had an artillery company made up of Germans and commanded by a German. The Confederacy recruited several companies of Germans in Richmond, Virginia, and Galveston raised a battalion made up of Germans. Fort Wagner in the harbor of Charleston, South Carolina, is named for General Wagner who entered the war as a colonel of artillery.

The Confederates do not seem to have indulged in much soul-searching over the issue of "foreign troops," perhaps because the Germans living in the southern states were, for the most part, old settlers. Nicola Marschall, who had been born in Prussia, designed the Confederate uniform and flag. Karl Gustav Memminger, who was born in Wurtemberg, was the Confederacy's secretary of the treasury.

PART IV.

German-Americans in the 20th Century

1. *World War I*

The outbreak of World War I in 1914 was the beginning of a great crisis for the German-American community. During the first three years of the war, the United States was neutral. Germany was then at war with England, France, and their allies. German-Americans at this time were to a great extent supporters of Germany's cause. Most of this support was found among the Germans who had immigrated to the United States since the end of the American Civil War. They had not completely lost their attachment to the "fatherland," as had the earlier German immigrants. German pride in the old country had increased with the unification of Germany in the 1870's, at which time a united Germany was created out of the group of small German states.

This feeling of nationalism seized even the Germans in America, and was fanned by hundreds of German-language American newspapers of the late 19th and early 20th century. By this time, German-Americans who could speak and write German well were beginning to disappear, so newspaper editors began to import their writers from Germany itself. These men lent an entirely new tone to the German-American press and their writing was often more concerned with admiring accounts of events in the Fatherland than with what was going on in America.

In the period before America entered the war, German-Americans tried hard to defend Germany from bitter Allied propaganda. When America declared war on Germany in 1917, the country went through a violent emotional reaction against Germany, German culture, and even American citizens of German origin. People were often unreasonable, and it is with a sense of shame that Americans now look back upon the anti-German feelings of those years. The study of the German language was dropped from public schools. Hundreds of German newspapers stopped publishing. German music was eliminated from opera and orchestral programs. German singing societies were disbanded. All things German were suspect, with the result that many ridiculous occurrences took place. Sauerkraut was given the new name of "liberty cabbage" and dachshunds were renamed "liberty hounds."

During the wave of anti-German feeling, many German families, some of whom had been in America for generations, changed their names. Businesses that made use of the word "German" changed

Madame Ernestine Schumann-Heink (left), a German-American opera singer. Madame Schumann-Heink's family was sharply divided during World War I but she remained loyal to her adopted country.

Winfield Scott Schley (right) served in the Civil War and the Spanish-American War. He became a rear admiral in 1899 and retired in 1901.

it to something else. "German-American" banks, for example, became "North American" banks. In St. Paul, Minnesota, the Germania Building, which housed the Germania Life Insurance Company of New York, changed its name to the Guardian Building and the huge statue of "Germania" which stood over the main entrance was hauled down.

There were heartbreaking divisions of loyalty among German-American families who had close relatives fighting on the German side. This happened to the beloved singer, Madame Ernestine Schumann-Heink, who was born in Bohemia, once a part of Germany. She came to America in 1898 to join the Metropolitan Opera Company, and became famous for her singing of German songs.

Madame Schumann-Heink had become an American citizen in 1908 but not all of her family had come over with her. During the war, some of her sons served in the German Army and one in the German Navy, while others served in the American Army. She herself remained loyal to her adopted country and entertained in army camps throughout the United States.

The German-Americans met the test of loyalty to their adopted country with honor and devotion. Thousands of men of German birth or ancestry fought bravely in the American Army. Their commander was one of the remarkable men of United States military history, General John J. Pershing, himself of old German ancestry, whose family had originally spelled their name Pfoerschin. Pershing, who was born in 1860, grew up in Missouri and attended the Military Academy at West Point, New York. He served in the Santiago campaign in Cuba during the Spanish-American War, where another German-American, Admiral Winfield Scott Schley, commanded the American naval forces. "Schley's Flying Squadron" was a famous unit in that war.

In 1916, Pershing, by then a brigadier general, was in charge of the American Army which campaigned along the Mexican border against the Mexican bandit, Francisco (Pancho) Villa. When America entered World War I, General Pershing was given command

General John J. Pershing, the descendant of early German immigrants. He commanded the American Expeditionary Force against Germany in World War I.

of the American Expeditionary Force. After the war, he held the highest rank which had ever been granted an officer in the American Army, General of the Armies of the United States. His book, *My Experiences in the World War,* won the Pulitzer prize for history in 1932. He died in 1948.

2. *German Immigration in the 20th Century*

The first 10 years of the 20th century saw a decline in German immigration. Although the number of immigrants in this period totaled 341,498, and was still large compared to the amount coming from other countries, it was the smallest number of Germans to come to the United States in 70 years. During the next 10 years, which was the period of the First World War, the number of German immigrants fell to the lowest level since the 1830's.

The years following the defeat of Germany in 1918 saw inflation, unemployment, and depression. German immigration to the United States in the 1920's increased almost three times over the previous 10 years. With the coming to power of Adolf Hitler at the beginning of the 1930's, immigration declined, but such immigration as there was took on a new character.

GERMAN IMMIGRATION IN THE 20TH CENTURY

1901-1910	341,498
1911-1920	143,945
1921-1930	412,202
1931-1940	114,058
1941-1950	226,578
1951-1960	477,765
1961	25,815
1962	21,477
1963	24,727
1964	24,494

The rise of the Nazi party in Germany ushered in one of the most terrible political and religious persecutions in the history of mankind. The main target of these attacks were German Jews, but they were not the only ones to suffer. All opponents of the Nazis were persecuted, including Protestant and Catholic religious leaders, leaders of other political parties, independent thinkers, university professors, trade unionists, and all who opposed the new regime. Many of these people fled Germany to save their lives, and this resulted in America receiving a new wave of "Forty-Eighters" — scientists, businessmen, writers, and scholars. Many of these refugees were Jews.

One of the most famous of the refugees and exiles was Albert Einstein, a physicist and a German Jew, who is regarded as one of the great thinkers of all time. He was born in 1879 at Ulm, Germany. When he was 15, he went to Switzerland, graduated from the University of Zurich, and became a Swiss citizen. He returned to Germany in 1913 as the director of the Kaiser Wilhelm Institute in Berlin and here, two years later, he announced his famous theory of relativity. He was awarded the Nobel prize in physics in 1921.

Einstein had been granted honorary German citizenship but in 1933, while on a lecture tour of England and the United States, Hitler revoked his German citizenship, stripped him of his position, and confiscated his property. Einstein then became director of the school of mathematics at the Institute for Advanced Study at Princeton, New Jersey. He became a naturalized American citizen in 1940.

In 1939, Einstein wrote the now-famous letter to President Franklin D. Roosevelt urging the need for research into the use of atomic energy for military purposes. He died in 1955.

Albert Einstein, the great physicist, who came to the United States as a refugee from Nazi Germany.

Paul Tillich, distinguished German Protestant theologian, who found refuge in the United States from Nazi persecution.

The famed Protestant theologian, Paul Tillich, was also a refugee from Hitler's Germany. The son of a Lutheran minister and a member of the Evangelical and Reformed Church, Tillich was born in Prussia. He left Germany in 1933 shortly after he was dismissed as professor of philosophy at the University of Frankfort-am-Main. An outspoken critic of Nazism, he later said:

> I had the great honor and luck to be the first non-Jewish professor dismissed from a German University.

After coming to the United States, Tillich taught at Harvard University, the Union Theological Seminary in New York City, and the Chicago Theological Seminary at the University of Chicago. His book, *Systematic Theology,* completed in 1963, has been called one of the major religious works of the 20th century. He wrote 15 books in English — a language he did not learn until he was 47 years old. He died in 1965.

Thomas Mann, the greatest modern German writer and one of the world's leading authors, was another refugee from the Nazis. He was born in Germany in 1875 and published his first important

Two of the great men of our time, both of whom were Nobel prize winners, and both refugees from Nazi Germany, are shown here. Albert Einstein (left) received the Nobel prize for physics. Thomas Mann (right) received the prize for literature. In the center is Rabbi Stephen Wise, an American active in assisting anti-Nazi refugees.

novel, *Buddenbrooks*, in 1900. His second book, *The Magic Mountain*, is considered one of the masterworks of the 20th century. On the basis of these writings, he was awarded the Nobel prize for literature in 1929.

Mann and his family were active anti-Nazis and his books were burned in Germany. He fled to Switzerland and later to the United States where he became an American citizen. His son, Klaus, a novelist and playwright who was a sergeant in the American Army during World War II, summed up the attitude of many German-Americans concerning the second war with Germany when he wrote:

> I am sure I speak for other Germans now active in the various forces of the United Nations when I say that our militant resolution has a two-fold psychological and moral source: first, our natural loyalty to the new homeland to which we are deeply indebted; and second, our intimate, first-hand knowledge of the mortal danger which Hitlerism means to civilization . . .

3. German-Americans and World War II

During World War II there was no anti-German hysteria, such as swept America during World War I. There was little real pro-Nazi feeling on the part of the great majority of Germans in America. One pro-Nazi German-American organization did exist, however, in the 1930's. This was the German-American Bund, led by Fritz Kuhn, a former chemical engineer who was "the American Fuhrer." Headquarters of the Bund were in "Yorkville," a section of New York City that had a large German population. The hard core of the Bund was made up of German-Americans who admired Hitler and his programs, but there were hundreds of members who were not German but shared the Bund's admiration for the German dictator. Kuhn and his "storm troopers" claimed a membership of 200,000, but one writer placed the number closer to 20,000. During the late 1930's, the Bund held rallies, made speeches, dressed in jackboots and Nazi swastika insignias, and marched carrying the Nazi swastika flag. When America entered World War II, the Bund collapsed. It was revived recently, a pale shadow of its former self, as the American Nazi party led by George Lincoln Rockwell who was not German at all.

During World War II, one writer estimates, approximately a third of the 11 million men and women who served in the American armed forces were of German and part-German ancestry. Three branches of the armed forces were led by men of German ancestry. General Eisenhower, who became Supreme Commander of the Allied forces in Europe, was descended from a family of German "sectarians" who settled in Pennsylvania in 1732. Like most "sectarians," the Eisenhowers originally were pacifists and his appointment to West Point and choice of the army as a career was a departure from the early traditions of the family.

General Carl Spaatz, of Pennsylvania Dutch origin, was Eisenhower's chief air advisor and planned the United States' bombing raids on Germany. Later in the war he was the European air commander, and then headed the strategic bombing force directed against Japan. After the war, he became the first chief of staff of the United States Air Force when, in 1947, it was separated from the army and made a separate branch of service.

Admiral Chester W. Nimitz was commander-in-chief of the United States Pacific fleet, taking over his command just a few weeks after the fleet had been badly damaged by the Japanese attack on Pearl Harbor. He directed the operations of both the Navy and the Marine Corps. In 1945, he was promoted to the rank of Admiral of the Fleet and after the war, became United States Chief of Naval Operations. General Walter Krueger, commander of the war in the Pacific, was born in Germany. Some writers estimate that about one-fifth of the approximately 3,500 American admirals and generals who served during World War II were of German ancestry.

When the first American division arrived in Europe, the first soldier to step off the ship when it docked at Belfast, Ireland, was Private William H. Henke of Hutchinson, Minnesota, whose parents were German immigrants. Alton Knapperberger was awarded the Congressional Medal of Honor for destroying two German machine gun nests and an anti-aircraft gun during the fighting at Anzio, in Italy. His family background was Pennsylvania Dutch, Mennonite, and pacifist.

General Dwight D. Eisenhower (left), Supreme Commander of the Allied Forces in Europe, and **General Carl Spaatz** (right), of the United States Air Force, were both descended from the Pennsylvania Dutch.

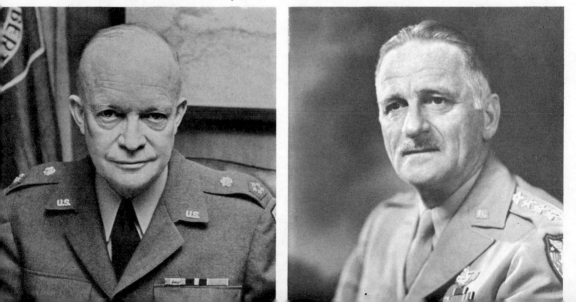

Herman Bottcher, who was born in Landsberg, Germany, was a major in the Abraham Lincoln brigade during the Spanish Civil War of the 1930's. When the United States entered World War II, he enlisted in the army and served in the South Pacific where he became known as a "one-man army." His bravery and military skill became legendary. After his death in action in 1944, he was awarded the Silver Star.

There were other contributions to the war effort by German-Americans. American troops crossed the Rhine River during the last month of the war and the amphibious tanks they used had been perfected by Donald Roebling, the great-grandson of John Roebling. Henry J. Kaiser, one of America's leading industrialists since the 1930's, was the son of a "Forty-Eighter." The mass-production techniques he introduced into shipbuilding helped America build up its fleet.

Admiral Chester W. Nimitz (right), Commander-in-Chief of the United States Pacific fleet, was another World War II American officer of German descent. He is shown here aboard a cruiser in Pearl Harbor, July, 1944, discussing the war with two other famous Americans who are descended from immigrants: **General Douglas MacArthur** (left), of Scotch-Irish ancestry, and **President Franklin Delano Roosevelt,** of French Huguenot and Dutch ancestry.

PART V.

Prominent German-Americans

Strange as it may seem, the story of the Germans in America has been one of contradictions. German immigrants were often considered plodders who cared little for education. Yet, they contributed greatly to the development of education in their new country. They were sometimes considered uncultured, but they contributed to the establishment of our country's cultural institutions, especially in the field of music. The great mass of Germans were often characterized as being uneducated. Some of America's greatest scientists, however, are German. Some of the country's most prosperous industries were founded by Germans and remain in the hands of their descendants even today. Yet, German immigrants have been thought of primarily as peasants and farmers.

Although many prominent individuals were mentioned throughout as the story of the German-Americans unfolded, there are still others whose contributions are worth listing. The following list, however, is far from complete.

1. *Industry*

John Jacob Bausch and Henry Lomb, two German immigrants, started a company in Rochester, New York, in 1849, which is internationally famous for its optical goods. Bausch was a skilled optician

John J. Bausch (left) and **Henry Lomb** (right), founders of a company long famous for a variety of optical goods.

and Lomb a business executive. The company went through many trying years, because of a common prejudice that American-made lenses were inferior to those made in Europe. Nevertheless, the company survived and prospered. By 1908 Bausch and Lomb was the largest lens manufacturer in the world, producing more than 20 million lenses annually for eyeglasses, cameras, microscopes, binoculars, and projectors.

John Augustus Roebling, who became famous as a bridge-builder, was a German immigrant. After graduating from the Royal

The Brooklyn Bridge in 1884, designed by a German immigrant, John Augustus Roebling. He was working on the Brooklyn Bridge at the time of his death. It was completed by his son, Washington Augustus Roebling.

John Augustus Roebling designed and built the first modern suspension bridges. He was also an accomplished musician and architect, besides being a great engineer.

Polytechnic Institute in Berlin, he moved to Pennsylvania. While working as a canal engineer, he was impressed by the lack of strong towropes. The standard tows were made from hemp and usually wore out rapidly. Roebling, after much experimentation, developed steel cable. In 1846, he completed the first suspension bridge at Pittsburgh, Pennsylvania. His greatest accomplishment was the construction of a suspension bridge at Niagara Falls, New York. This giant structure was 821 feet long and for nearly 50 years it held up under the strain of heavy train traffic.

At the time of his death, Roebling was working on the gigantic Brooklyn Bridge over the East River in New York City. His son, Washington Augustus Roebling, who was also a famous engineer, completed the bridge. John Roebling is remembered for revolutionizing bridge-building and also for establishing the firm of John A. Roebling's Sons, which became the most important manufacturer of steel cable in the nation.

August Belmont was a banker when he emigrated to America. Born at Alzei, Germany, Belmont went to work for the Rothschild banking house when he was 14 years old. Upon moving to the United States, he started the banking firm of August Belmont and Company in New York City. Within a few years he was one of the leading bankers in the nation.

August Belmont, who was born in Prussia, became an American banker and diplomat.

Henry Englehard Steinweg, founder of the famous Steinway Piano Company.

Belmont was a prominent Democrat, and he served as United States consul general to Austria between 1844 and 1850, and as United States minister to The Netherlands from 1853 to 1867. He enthusiastically supported the Northern cause during the War Between the States and was instrumental in bringing many European financial and political leaders to the support of the Union.

Henry Engelhard Steinweg began making pianos in the kitchen of his house in a tiny mountain town in Germany. Then he moved to the United States, modified his name to Steinway, and soon he and his sons were putting together pianos in a loft in New York City. His daughter sold them as fast as they were finished by offering free piano lessons to prospective customers, and so the firm of Steinway & Sons was born.

The number of American manufacturers of musical instruments who were German is surprising. Besides Steinway, there were Knabe, Wurlitzer, Weber, and Gemunder, to mention just a few. These names are still prominent.

The Studebaker brothers, Henry and Clement, opened a wagon-building and blacksmith's shop in 1852 in South Bend, Indiana, with an initial investment of $68. Their first large order, 100 wagons for the United States Army, came in 1857. In 1858 another brother, John, joined them, investing $8,000 he had earned building wheelbarrows in the California goldfields. During the Civil War, the

The Studebaker brothers. Henry (left) and Clem (center) founded the well-known Studebaker Corporation in 1852 with an investment of $68. Later, the other brothers joined the business.

Studebakers produced chuck wagons, transports, ambulances, and artillery equipment for the Union Army. By 1895 they were the world's largest wagon producers, turning out 75,000 horse-drawn vehicles every year. Then came the horseless carriage. In 1919, having made gun carriages, artillery wheels, escort wagons, tank wagons, and ambulances for the army during World War I, the company discontinued all wagon production to concentrate on automobiles. Today the Studebaker Corporation is a large diversified manufacturing company, but is no longer in the automobile business.

August A. Busch, Jr., president of the Anheuser-Busch Company, a leading American brewery. Germans were the most important group in the beer industry.

67

German names seem to have dominated the early years of the brewing industry, and still do, for that matter — Pabst, Anheuser-Busch, Schlitz, Schmidt, Hamm, Pfeiffer, Blatz, Kunz. In the food industry, there are Heinz, Hershey, Kraft, and Fleischmann, to mention just a few.

Henry J. Heinz, who was born in Pittsburgh, Pennsylvania, in 1844, was descended from German immigrants. While working in his father's brickyard, he began marketing garden surplus. When he was only 16 he had his own hotbeds and was raising and distributing vegetables. When he was 25 he helped organize a business to market grated horseradish. When this failed, he turned to the manufacturing of pickles, spices, relishes, and other prepared foods. The famous slogan, "57 Varieties," was originated by Heinz in 1896. Actually his company made more than 57 products but he liked the sound of 57 and regarded it as his lucky number. By the time of his death in 1919, the H. J. Heinz Company employed over 6,000 people and had 25 branch offices. The company operated its own bottle, box, and can factories, and also its own seed and vegetable farms.

Frederick Weyerhaeuser, founder of the Weyerhaeuser Lumber Company, prominent American lumber and forest products concern.

Frederick Weyerhaeuser, one of 11 children of a humble German farm family, was another of America's industrial giants. He was born in 1834 and as a teen-ager accompanied his family to the United States. His first job was as a laborer in Pennsylvania. After moving to Illinois he worked in a lumberyard. During the 1860's he went from the lumberyard business into the sawmill business. Because he found it desirable to have his own timberlands in order to have a good supply of lumber, Weyerhaeuser expanded his operations by purchasing forests first in Wisconsin and then in Minnesota.

During the 1880's, Weyerhaeuser's company was one of the largest timber cutters in Wisconsin. In the 1890's when Minnesota became a ranking lumber state, he moved to St. Paul. While in Minnesota, he expanded his operations to include railroading and banking. In the early 20th century, Weyerhaeuser extended his business into the Pacific Northwest and portions of the South. The company that bears his name is still one of the main producers and distributors of lumber products in the United States.

The publishing business also was expanding rapidly during these years between the Civil War and World War I and German

Ottmar Mergenthaler (seated) and Whitelaw Reid at *The New York Tribune*. In July 1886, Mergenthaler's first commercial linotype was installed at *The New York Tribune*. This machine helped speed the process of setting type.

names were prominent in this field, too. The man who perhaps did more than any other one person for the printing industry of this period was Ottmar Mergenthaler, who invented the linotype machine, a fast, dependable mechanical process for composing type. Mergenthaler was a schoolmaster's son and he was born in 1854 in the village of Hachtel, Germany. Unable to go to high school because his family was poor, he was apprenticed at the age of 14 to a watchmaker. When he was 18, he came to America and went to work in the Washington shop of his cousin, building models for inventors seeking patents. Here he became aware of the problem facing the printing industry, the need for a newer and faster way of setting type. After 14 years of experimenting, he developed the first commercial linotype which was installed at the *New York Tribune* on July 3, 1886. By 1890, Mergenthaler had established his own factory in Brooklyn.

Henry Villard was a journalist and a railroad financier. As a young man of 18, he moved to New York and became a newspaper reporter. During the 1870's, Villard was an important figure in the formation of several railroads. He also was owner of the *New York Evening Post* and Carl Schurz was one of his editors for a time. Villard gave financial support to Thomas A. Edison and helped found the Edison General Electric Company, predecessor of the present General Electric Company. He died in 1900.

Henry Villard, president of the Northern Pacific Railroad when its first transcontinental line was completed in 1883. This line linked Lake Superior with Puget Sound.

Henry Clay Frick, founder of the Frick Coal and Iron Company. He was an important industrialist and a director of several railroads and the United States Steel Corporation.

John D. Rockefeller, founder of the Standard Oil Company. The first American Rockefeller immigrated from Germany in the 1720's, but by the time John D. was born he was only about "three-sixteenths" German. The Rockefeller family have been prominent philanthropists. They have contributed millions for education, science, and health through the famed Rockefeller Foundation.

Two prominent merchants of German-Jewish extraction were Benjamin Altman and Nathan Straus. Altman founded a famous New York department store, and Straus, who was born in Otterberg, Germany, developed Macy's in New York, probably the best known store in the United States. John Wanamaker was another American merchant of German ancestry. He founded the large Philadelphia store which bears his name.

American business and industry are indebted to many others of German ancestry. They cannot all be listed, but among the most prominent are Claus Spreckels, the sugar refiner, Charles Schwab and Henry Clay Frick, the coal, iron, and steel magnates, and Seiberling, the tire-maker. Walter P. Chrysler, founder of the automobile company bearing his name, was also of German descent.

The Rockefeller family, which is so prominent in American life, is descended from Johann Peter Rockefeller who came to America from the Rhineland country of Germany in the early 1720's. However, one historian says that John D. Rockefeller, who was born in 1839 and founded both the Standard Oil Company and the

An early Standard Oil filling station. Oil and gas were the basis of Rockefeller wealth, one of the greatest fortunes ever built.

family fortune, had "three-sixteenths or less" of German blood. This illustrates quite clearly the mixing and blending of the American "melting pot."

2. *Education*

The Germans who came to the United States made at least three outstanding contributions to the nation's educational system. Mrs. Carl Schurz was a pioneer in children's education in America. She organized the first kindergarten in the country at Watertown, Wisconsin, in the 1850's. By 1873, kindergartens were popular enough to cause the St. Louis, Missouri, school board to establish a public kindergarten system. Nearly all of the first kindergarten teachers were German immigrants.

Because of their skill as craftsmen, the Germans were also interested in seeing a system of vocational training set up and they pioneered in this field. The beginning of trade schools in the United States was mainly sponsored by German immigrants.

A third contribution was physical education. The Germans, more than any other group, emphasized the importance of physical education in school programs. The inspiration for physical training came mainly from the German Turner societies. These societies were first organized in Germany during the Napoleonic era for the purpose of developing German patriotism by stressing physical education and strength. As these gymnastic societies grew, they emphasized both physical and mental improvement.

The first Turner societies were organized in the United States in 1848, and the Turners dedicated their first American hall two years later in Cincinnati, Ohio. Within a few years there were 60 societies in the nation, all led by instructors who had received their physical education in Germany. Largely because of the Turners, physical education was added to many public school curriculums, and some schools started gymnastic programs. In 1875 the Turners founded a normal school in Milwaukee for the purpose of training physical education instructors.

Another aspect of the Germans' impact on education was the emphasis the German Lutheran Church and the Roman Catholic Church placed upon parochial schools.

There were also many liberal Germans in education. Felix Adler, a teacher, reformer, and founder of the Ethical Culture movement, was German. So was Maximilian Berlitz, founder of the language schools which now dot the country. The "free-thinkers" among the Germans, who were usually non-religious, favored a system of private schools. As the American public school system developed, private schools decreased. Many Germans,

An early American kindergarten. This school for young children is a German contribution to American education. The word kindergarten means "child's garden," or play-place.

Professor Maximilian Berlitz, founder of the Berlitz Schools, was famous both nationally and internationally. This picture shows him giving a group of Paris policemen a lesson in English to prepare them for the visit of Edward VII of England.

however, anxious to preserve their culture, which they often felt was superior to that of America, began to press for the teaching of the German language in the public schools. In many states, German influence was large enough to have this proposal adopted and the teaching of German became a part of the public school curriculum until World War I. German is again widely taught today.

Reinhold Niebuhr, theologian and educator, is one of the outstanding religious philosophers in the world today. The son of a German immigrant, he was born in Wright City, Missouri, in 1892 and graduated from Yale Divinity School. Throughout his career Niebuhr has shown great concern for social justice and labor reform. He became dean of Union Theological Seminary in New York City in 1950.

3. *Science and Medicine*

During much of the 19th century, American science, including medicine, was not as advanced as that of Europe. In Europe, Germany had led the way in the development of modern science. Thus, many branches of medicine in the United States were deeply influenced by German immigrants. German pharmacists were unique because they had training in chemistry. By the middle 1800's, German pharmacists were found throughout the United States. One of them, Johann Michael Maisch, was professor of

Reinhold Niebuhr, son of a German immigrant, is one of the world's noted religious philosophers.

pharmacy in the New York College of Pharmacy, and served during the Civil War as supervisor of the Union Army Medical Laboratory which produced medicines for the military forces.

In addition to practicing pharmacy, some of the Germans pioneered in the manufacturing of drugs. Two brothers, Drs. Louis and Charles E. Dohme, founded the firm which now is Merck, Sharp, and Dohme, one of the largest pharmaceutical companies in America.

Among the German immigrants were many doctors. They had fine reputations and were among the leaders in improving American medical training and practice. In an era when general practice was the rule, some of the Germans were skilled specialists. Dr.

Charles P. Steinmetz was born in Germany in 1865 and came to the United States in 1889. He made many contributions to the world of electrical science.

Albert Abraham Michelson, an outstanding German-born physicist and Nobel prize winner, made important discoveries in the field of light. He headed the Department of Physics at the University of Chicago.

Dr. Wernher von Braun, a German-born rocket expert who helps direct American missile and space program. He became a citizen in 1958.

Abraham Jacobi, for example, was a famous pediatrician and authority on children's diseases and infant feeding. He opened the United States' first free clinic for treatment of children's diseases and published eight volumes on medicine. Dr. Simon Baruch, who had been assistant surgeon for the Confederate Army, improved surgery methods, particularly for appendicitis. He was the father of Bernard Baruch, financier and statesman. Dr. Gustav Bruhl was an important throat specialist.

The famous German-American scientist Charles Proteus Steinmetz was born in Breslau, Germany, in 1865. He became the genius behind the development of the General Electric Corporation. His laboratory was at Schenectady, New York, and he became known as "The Wizard of Schenectady." Steinmetz was a small crippled man, scarcely over four feet tall. An ardent socialist, he had to flee Germany because of an editorial he wrote for a socialist newspaper.

Steinmetz came to the United States in 1889 and during the next 25 years became one of the world's top-ranking inventors. He has been given credit for more than 100 inventions necessary in the use of electricity. His most dramatic experiment was made in 1921 when he created man-made lightning in his laboratory to learn how to protect electrical systems from being damaged by lightning.

Albert Abraham Michelson, a physicist who was a graduate of the United States Naval Academy, won the Nobel prize in 1907 for research which contributed to the understanding of the speed of light and the curvature of light rays. Other Nobel prize winners were Isidor Isaac Rabi, also in physics, and Karl Landsheimer in medicine.

Wernher von Braun, an engineer and rocket expert, was born in Germany in 1912 and studied engineering in Berlin and Zurich, Switzerland. During World War II, he headed Germany's missile program, but was captured by the American Army in 1945. He then came to White Sands, New Mexico, to help the United States Army experiment with missiles and in 1950 was made head of the Army Ordinance Guided Missile Center in Alabama. Von Braun became an American citizen in 1958. In recent years, he has been a key leader in the development of the United States space program and has contributed much to the development of rocket design, motors, and liquid fuel.

4. *Government and Politics*

The best known German-American political figure of the 19th century after Carl Schurz, was John Peter Altgeld, governor of Illinois. Altgeld had little formal education and worked for years as a laborer, but he studied law and was elected state's attorney for a Missouri county in 1874. He later moved to Chicago and became prominent in the Democratic party. In 1892 he was elected to a four-year term as governor of Illinois, the first foreign-born person to hold that office. It is believed that he would have been the Democratic nominee for President if he had not been legally barred by his foreign birth.

One man, not himself a politician, should perhaps be mentioned here. He is Thomas Nast, the famous cartoonist, who originated two of America's best known symbols, the Republican elephant and the Democratic donkey. He was born in Germany in 1840 and brought to New York by his mother when he was only six years old. As a boy he pursued his great love for drawing, and at 15 he was employed by *Frank Leslie's Illustrated Newspaper* to do sketches. During the Civil War he worked for *Harper's Weekly*. Lincoln called him the Union's best recruiter. Following the war, Nast bitterly attacked the notorious political leaders of New York through his cartoons. The famous donkey and elephant were both well-fixed in his pictures by 1874. Nast died in 1902.

The first man of German descent to be elected President of the United States was Herbert Hoover in 1928. He was born in

The Herbert Hoover commemorative postage stamp. It was issued in 1965, shortly after the death of our 31st President. Hoover was the first Quaker ever to be elected to the Presidency. He began his career as a mining engineer, and became wealthy. Much of his life was spent working for humanitarian goals.

West Branch, Iowa, in 1874, and made a large fortune as a mining engineer. In the years following World War I, Hoover headed the American Relief Administration, and received world fame for his efforts to help the suffering people of Europe. The Republican Convention of 1928 nominated him on the first ballot as their party's candidate for President.

The election of 1928 had some interesting aspects. Hoover was not only the first man of German ancestry, but also the first Quaker to be elected President. His Democratic opponent, Governor Alfred E. Smith, was the first presidential candidate who was of Irish-Catholic descent.

Wendell L. Willkie was the Republican candidate for President in 1940. He once remarked that his grandparents had left Germany as "protestants against autocracy." The family name had originally been spelled "Willicke."

The second American President of German descent was Dwight D. Eisenhower. His ancestors had come to Pennsylvania in 1732. He was born in Texas in 1890 and raised in Abilene, Kansas. After graduating from West Point in 1915 he followed a military career that led to the position of Supreme Commander of all the Allied

Dwight D. Eisenhower, of Pennsylvania Dutch descent, served two terms as the 34th President of the United States. During his administration, from 1952-1960, the Korean War was ended, the United States launched its first satellite, and Alaska and Hawaii were admitted to the Union.

Forces in Europe in World War II. It was an interesting coincidence of history that the two men who led the United States armies in both of America's wars with Germany were men of German ancestry—Pershing and Eisenhower.

Following World War II, Eisenhower was Army Chief of Staff. Upon retirement he was appointed president of Columbia University. In 1952 he was the first Republican candidate to be elected President in 20 years. He was re-elected in 1956. From 1961 until his death in 1969, Eisenhower served as an elder statesman for his party and his country.

There have been numerous other prominent individuals of German ancestry on the political scene. Senator William E. Borah of Idaho was a descendant of Catherine von Borah, the wife of Martin Luther. Robert F. Wagner, Sr., of New York was a German immigrant who became a New York Supreme Court judge and then a United States senator. He gave his name to the Wagner Act, the federal act establishing the National Labor Relations Board. His son, Robert F. Wagner, Jr., was elected mayor of New York City in 1954—the city's 102nd mayor. He held this post until 1965, and in 1968 was appointed ambassador to Spain.

Bernard Baruch, advisor to eight United States Presidents, beginning with Woodrow Wilson and ending with John F. Kennedy, was the son of the famed Confederate surgeon, Dr. Simon Baruch. His father, who was born in Germany, came from a family which

Governor Nelson H. Rockefeller of New York, the grandson of John D. Rockefeller. The Rockefeller family today is active in politics and public service.

Henry Kissinger, President Nixon's assistant for National Security Affairs. Kissinger, who came to America from Germany in 1938, has taught at Harvard University.

Bernard Baruch, statesman and advisor to eight Presidents from Woodrow Wilson to John F. Kennedy. He is shown here with another prominent friend, British Prime Minister Winston Churchill.

traced its ancestry back to the Jews of Spain and Portugal. Baruch began his business career as a clerk and had become a wealthy man by the time he was 30 years of age. He became interested in government and philanthropy, and President Wilson, recognizing his ability, named him director of the War Industries Board in World War I. This was the only major government position Baruch ever held. After World War II, he was the United States representative to the United Nations Atomic Energy Commission. He proposed the development of an international atomic control authority as the best way to assure world peace. Baruch gave millions of dollars to charity, relief organizations, hospitals, and schools. He died in 1965.

5. *Sports and Entertainment*

German names in the entertainment world include movie director Ernst Lubitsch; actor-director Erich von Stroheim, who is remembered particularly for his roles as Nazi officers; movie actress Marlene Dietrich. Theatrical producer Florenz Ziegfeld was famed in the 1920's for his "Ziegfeld Follies." He was born in Chicago where his German immigrant father directed the Chicago Musical College. Florenz Ziegfeld's musical revues glorified the American girl and influenced American fashions.

Marlene Dietrich, glamorous German-born film star.

Florenz Ziegfeld, noted theatrical producer.

There are many German names in the field of sports, including Babe Ruth, Honus Wagner, Heinie Manush, Red Schoendienst, and Lou Gehrig. Some of America's greatest swimmers have been of German ancestry. Among them are Johnny Weissmuller, the movies' best known and most popular "Tarzan," and Gertrude Ederle who, on August 6, 1926, became the first woman to swim the English Channel.

George Herman (Babe) Ruth   **Honus Wagner**   **Henry Louis Gehrig**

GEORGE HERMAN (BABE) RUTH
BOSTON-NEW YORK, A.L.; BOSTON, N.L.
1915 - 1935
GREATEST DRAWING CARD IN HISTORY OF
BASEBALL. HOLDER OF MANY HOME RUN
AND OTHER BATTING RECORDS. GATHERED
714 HOME RUNS IN ADDITION TO FIFTEEN
IN WORLD SERIES.

HONUS WAGNER
LOUISVILLE, N.L. 1897-1899.
PITTSBURGH, N.L. 1900-1917.
THE GREATEST SHORTSTOP IN BASEBALL
HISTORY. BORN CARNEGIE, Pa., FEB. 24, 1874
KNOWN TO FAME AS "HONUS", "HANS" AND
"THE FLYING DUTCHMAN." RETIRED IN 1917,
HAVING SCORED MORE RUNS, MADE MORE
HITS AND STOLEN MORE BASES THAN
ANY OTHER PLAYER IN THE HISTORY
OF HIS LEAGUE.

HENRY LOUIS GEHRIG
NEW YORK YANKEES 1923-1939
HOLDER OF MORE THAN A SCORE OF
MAJOR AND AMERICAN LEAGUE RECORDS,
INCLUDING THAT OF PLAYING 2130
CONSECUTIVE GAMES. WHEN HE RETIRED
IN 1939, HE HAD A LIFE TIME BATTING
AVERAGE OF .340.

6. *Music and Literature*

The German passion for music has greatly enriched American life. English colonists, particularly the Puritans, regarded music as frivolous and unnecessary. The informal, fun-loving Germans, however, pioneered in introducing both formal and folk music. The beginnings of the great choral societies and other singing groups of today can be traced to German federations of singing societies. These groups commonly entertained at public celebrations, such as the Fourth of July. The Germans also were the leaders in establishing chamber music ensembles and symphony orchestras. And little German bands were an institution in any area where Germans were found.

In 1848, 23 German refugees in New York City founded the Germania Orchestra, one of the first symphony orchestras in America. They toured the country for six years, giving 800 concerts. They not only introduced the works of such composers as Beethoven and Wagner to American audiences but they inspired

John Philip Sousa was partly of German descent. He was known as the "March King." "The Stars and Stripes Forever" and "Washington Post March" are especially famous and popular.

Theodore Dreiser, one of America's first realistic novelists. His most noted work is *An American Tragedy*. He was born in Terre Haute, Indiana, in 1871 and died in 1945.

other Americans to form orchestras, too. Nearly all the members of the Germania Orchestra eventually became conductors or concertmasters of new orchestras. Later, there were such men as Leopold Damrosch, the violinist, conductor, and founder of the New York Symphony Society and the New York Oratorio Society. His son, Walter Johannes Damrosch, a conductor and composer, was widely known for popularizing music through the medium of radio broadcasts. Frederick Stock, Bruno Walter, and Emil Oberhoffer, were all conductors of German origin. John Philip Sousa, "the March King" and America's most famous composer of band music, was partly of German descent.

Literary figures of German descent include H. L. Mencken, John Gunther, Emil Ludwig, John Steinbeck, and Theodore Dreiser, to mention only a few. Dreiser began his writing career as a newspaper reporter and magazine editor in Chicago and New York. His concern for individuals and social justice helped him become one of America's first realistic novelists. Two of his outstanding works are *Sister Carrie* and *An American Tragedy*.

On a visit to West Berlin, novelist **John Steinbeck** (right) speaks with Willy Brandt, then mayor of the city. Steinbeck, who died in 1968, is best known for his novel *Grapes of Wrath*. Awarded the Nobel prize for literature in 1962, he was the sixth American to win this high literary honor.

CONCLUSION

It has been estimated that from one in six to one in every four Americans is of German descent. The impact of the German immigration upon America cannot be exaggerated. One of the Germans' most endearing contributions to American life has been the celebration of Christmas as we know it today. It is difficult to realize that the so-called typical American Christmas has not always been a part of American life. New England Puritans did not celebrate Christmas and in many sections of the United States, as late as the Civil War, this special day was observed in Halloween fashion, with mischief and rowdyism. The Pennsylvania Dutch and the colonial Swedes both considered Christmas a church day and both used Christmas trees, but it was the 19th century German immigrants who changed the nature of Christmas throughout the nation. They popularized Christmas as a religious observance. In the early 1830's, German immigrants introduced the gaily-decorated Christmas trees. Some of the loveliest Christmas carols, such as *Silent Night,* are a heritage from the Germans.

German food also has become an inseparable part of American life — wieners, frankfurters, hamburgers, sauerkraut, liverwurst, noodles, schnitzel, pumpernickel, zweiback, and pretzels.

The English language has been enriched by new words introduced by the Germans — gesundheit, kindergarten, delicatessen, nix, ouch, dumb, ya, and hausfrau. Many words are a combination of English words with German endings. The most common German suffixes, or endings, are -fest, -lust, and -burger. So, today we have such words as songfest and slugfest, hamburger and cheeseburger, wanderlust and squanderlust.

Sometimes disliked, often misunderstood, occasionally the victims of suspicion, but also greatly admired as they put down their roots in American soil — these were the Germans who came to America and gave their new country their devotion and loyalty, their sturdiness and common sense, their talent, their thriftiness, their business insight, and their love of life.

ACKNOWLEDGEMENTS

The Illustrations are reproduced through the courtesy of: pp. 6, 13, 16, 18, 23, 28, 32 (bottom), 36, 43, 53 (left), 55, 61 (left), 62, 64 (bottom), 65, 73, 79, 82 (top right), 83 (left), Independent Picture Service; p. 10, The Metropolitan Museum of Art; p. 20, The Smithsonian Institution; pp. 29, 31, 35, 57, 66 (left), 70 (right), 76 (left), Library of Congress; pp. 30, 78, Post Office Department, Division of Philately; pp. 32, 53 (right), United States Navy; pp. 34, 70 (left), Northern Pacific Railway Company; p. 37, New York Public Library; pp. 38, 45, Oregon State Highway Department; p. 40, Minnesota State Historical Society; p. 41, United States Immigration and Naturalization Service; pp. 48 (left), 49 (left and right), 51 (left and right), National Archives; p. 48 (right), New York City Department of Parks; pp. 58, 75 (top), Union Theological Seminary; pp. 59, 83 (right), 84, Wide World Photos; p. 61 (right), United States Army; p. 64 (top), Bausch and Lomb, Inc.; p. 66 (right), Steinway Company; p. 67 (top), The Studebaker Company; p. 67 (bottom), Anheuser Busch, Inc.; p. 68, Weyerhaeuser Company; p. 69, Mergenthaler Linotype Company; pp. 71, 72, Standard Oil Company; p. 74, Berlitz Schools of Languages; p. 75 (bottom), General Electric Company; p. 76 (right), National Aeronautics and Space Administration; p. 77, Illinois State Historical Library; p. 80 (left), Office of the Governor; p. 80 (right) Henry Kissinger; p. 81, Holt, Rinehard and Winston, Inc.; p. 82 (top left), TV Times; p. 82 (bottom), National Baseball Hall of Fame.

ABOUT THE AUTHOR . . .

VIRGINIA BRAINARD KUNZ is a native Minnesotan whose roots reach deep into America's past. Her first American forebear, Daniel Brainard, came to Massachusetts from England in 1649 and married a descendant of the Pilgrims who were on the *Mayflower*. Later Brainards went west, and Mrs. Kunz's great-grandfather Oliver Brainard II, arrived in Minnesota in 1866. On the maternal side, her great-grandfather was born in Norway and immigrated to Minnesota. Her grandfather married into a French-Canadian family that immigrated to Quebec in 1690. The grandfather of Mrs. Kunz's husband came to the United States from Germany in the 1860's. She, herself, graduated in 1943 from Iowa State University, and embarked upon a journalism career with the Minneapolis newspapers the *Star* and the *Tribune*. At present she is Executive Secretary of the Ramsey County Historical Society and editor of the journal, *Ramsey County History*. She is also a free lance writer, and author of *Muskets to Missiles: A Military History of Minnesota*. She is listed in *Who's Who of American Women*, *Who's Who in the Midwest* and *Who's Who in Minnesota*. Mrs. Kunz, her husband, and their two children, reside in Minneapolis.

The IN AMERICA *Series*

We specialize in publishing quality books for
young people. For a complete list please write:

LERNER PUBLICATIONS COMPANY
241 First Avenue North, Minneapolis, Minnesota 55401